Halloween Recipes

Hannie P. Scott

www.Hanniepscott.com

www.Hanniepscott.com

MY FREE GIFT TO YOU!

55 Quick & Easy Recipes

hannie p. scott

To download your free gift, simply visit:

www.hanniepscott.com/freegift

TABLE OF CONTENTS

For more books by Hannie, please visit:
www.Hanniepscott.com/books

ABBREVIATIONS

oz = ounce

fl oz = fluid ounce

tsp = teaspoon

tbsp = tablespoon

ml = milliliter

c = cup

pt = pint

qt = quart

gal = gallon

L = liter

CONVERSIONS

1/2 fl oz = 3 tsp = 1 tbsp = 15 ml

1 fl oz = 2 tbsp = 1/8 c = 30 ml

2 fl oz = 4 tbsp = 1/4 c = 60 ml

4 fl oz = 8 tbsp = 1/2 c = 118 ml

8 fl oz = 16 tbsp = 1 c = 236 ml

16 fl oz = 1 pt = 1/2 qt = 2 c = 473 ml

128 fl oz = 8 pt = 4 qt = 1 gal = 3.78 L

DRINKS

Apple Pie Smoothie

Servings: 2

What you need:

- · 2 cups nonfat Greek yogurt
- · 3/4 cup applesauce
- · 1 apple; peeled, cored, and diced
- · 1/2 tsp cinnamon
- · 1/4 tsp ground nutmeg

What to do:

1. Combine all ingredients in a blender and blend until smooth.
2. Pour into glasses and serve.

FiZZY BlOOd SmOOthie

Servings: 1-2

What you need:

- 1 cup Sprite
- 1 1/2 cups lemonade
- 1 cup frozen raspberries
- 1/2 cup frozen strawberries
- 1 cup raspberry sherbet

What to do:

1. Combine all ingredients in a blender and blend until smooth.
2. Pour into glasses and serve.

Halloween Punch

Servings: 1

What you need:

- 8 oz V8 peach mango
- 6 oz Peach flavored soda
- 1 scoop mango sherbet

What to do:

1. Pour the V8 and soda in a glass then add the scoop of sherbet.
2. Enjoy!

Blood Orange Smoothie

Servings: 1-2

What you need:

- 2 cups carrot juice
- 1/2 cup orange juice
- 2 blood oranges, peeled
- 1 cup nonfat Greek yogurt
- 6 ice cubes

What to do:

1. Combine all ingredients in a blender and blend until smooth.
2. Pour into glasses and serve.

Witch's Potion

Servings: 16

What you need:

- · 1 quart lime sherbet
- · 2 liter ginger ale
- · 2 cups pineapple juice
- · Green food coloring
- · Gummy worms

What to do:

1. Add all of the ingredients to a punch bowl except the sherbet and worms.
2. Right before serving, spoon in the sherbet and garnish the punch bowl or the individual cups with the gummy worms.

Vampire Hot Chocolate

Servings: 4

What you need:

Hot chocolate:

- 3 cups whole milk
- 1 cup heavy cream
- 1 tsp vanilla extract
- 8-oz white chocolate chips
- 1/2 cup mini chocolate chips
- Red food coloring

Whipped cream:

- 1 tsp vanilla extract
- 1 tbsp powdered sugar
- 1 cup heavy whipping cream

What to do:

1. In the bowl of a mixer, add 1 cup of heavy cream, vanilla, and powdered sugar. Whip on medium until stiff peaks form.
2. In a medium saucepan, add the whole milk, heavy cream, vanilla, white chocolate chips, and mini chocolate chips.
3. Heat over medium-low, stirring occasionally, until the chocolate is melted and begins to simmer but don't let it boil.
4. Stir in a couple drops of red food coloring.

5. Pour the hot chocolate into 4 mugs and top with whipped cream.

Jack O'Lantern Float

Servings: 6-10

What you need:

- 2 liters of orange soda
- 1 container orange sherbet
- Clear plastic cups

What to do:

1. Using a black permanent market, draw Jack O'Lantern eyes, nose, and mouth on the clear plastic cups.
2. Place a scoopful of orange sherbet into each cup.
3. Pour orange soda over the sherbet.

Fog Punch

Servings: varies

What you need:

- Blue Hawaiian punch
- Green Gatorade
- 1 liter of ginger ale
- Gummy worms
- Dry Ice

What to do:

1. You can adjust the amounts of ingredients used according to how much punch you want to use.
2. Fill your punch bowl with Hawaiian punch, Gatorade, and ginger ale.
3. Add gummy worms around the edges of the punch bowl (or to the individual glasses).
4. Using gloves, add a few small pieces of dry ice to make the fog. Before handling dry ice, make sure you are familiar with proper safety precautions.

Halloween Hot Chocolate

Servings: 1

What you need:

- 10-15 mini marshmallows
- Black food coloring marker
- 1 serving of hot chocolate

What to do:

1. Color ghost faces on each marshmallow. I like to do the eyes and then a big "O" mouth.
2. Make the hot chocolate.
3. Serve the hot chocolate with the marshmallows in it.

***This is a fun way to surprise your little ones OR a fun project to do together!

Bloody Halloween Punch

Servings: 15

What you need:

- 1/2 gallon of Hawaiian Punch
- 1 3-oz box of cherry Jello
- 1 cup of water
- 3 cups ginger ale

What to do:

1. Pour Hawaiian Punch into a large pitcher.
2. Bring the water to a boil and mix in the Jello. Stir for 1-2 minutes or until dissolved.
3. Pour the Jello mix into the Hawaiian Punch and stir well.
4. Carefully pour the mixture into ice cube trays and freeze.
5. Before serving, place the frozen cubes into a large glass pitcher. Pour in the ginger ale and stir until slushy.

CAKES & COOKIES

candy corn Devil's Food cake

Servings: 12

What you need:

· 1 box Devil's food cake mix, plus ingredients box calls for
· 1 can of sweetened condensed milk
· 16-oz whipped cream, thawed
· 1 cup caramel ice cream topping
· 2 cups candy corn

What to do:

1. Mix and bake the cake according to box directions in a 9x13 inch dish. Let cool for 10 minutes.
2. Poke holes all over the cake with the end of a wooden spoon.
3. Pour the sweetened condensed milk and caramel over the cake, making sure they go into the holes.
4. Cover and refrigerate the cake for 1 hour or until it is cool.
5. Top the cake with whipped cream.
6. Sprinkle candy corn over the whipped cream.

candy corn poke cake

Servings: 8-10

What you need:

- 1 box white cake mix, plus the ingredients the box calls for
- 14-oz can sweetened condensed milk
- Yellow and orange food coloring
- 16 oz tub of whipped cream, thawed
- Candy corn

What to do:

1. Mix the cake according to the box directions then evenly divide the cake mix into two separate bowls.
2. Using the food coloring, dye one bowl of batter yellow and one orange.
3. Grease a 9x13 inch baking dish with nonstick spray and spread the yellow cake batter across the bottom.
4. Cover and put the dish in the freezer for 30 minutes.
5. Remove the dish from the freezer and gently pour the orange batter over the yellow and carefully spread it evenly.
6. Bake the cake according to the package directions or until a toothpick inserted comes out clean. It may take a few extra minutes since the cake batter was slightly frozen.
7. Remove the cake from the oven and poke holes all over it with the end of a wooden spoon.
8. Pour the sweetened condensed milk evenly into the holes and all over the cake.
9. Place the cake in the refrigerator for at least 2 hours.

10. Before serving the cake, evenly spread the whipped cream over it.
11. Top the whipped cream with candy corns.

Frankenstein cupcakes

Servings: 8-10

What you need:

- 1 cake mix (your choice of what kind)
- Additional ingredients the cake mix calls for
- Green ice cream cones
- 1 container chocolate icing
- Black icing gel
- Smarties candies

What to do:

1. Prepare the cake mix according to the directions on the box.
2. Place ice cream cones in a muffin pan. One in each spot.
3. Fill the cones 2/3 full with cake batter.
4. Bake according to cake mix directions or until a toothpick inserted comes out clean.
5. Let them cool completely.
6. For Frankenstein's bolts, stick together two smarties candies with a small amount of the chocolate icing. Apply a little more icing to the sides of the cone and stick the "bolts" onto the cone. You need one bolt on each side of the cone.
7. Ice the tops of the cupcakes with chocolate icing.
8. Use the black icing gel to make Frankenstein's face and add some stitches to his head.

caramel Apple Dump cake

Servings: 8-10

What you need:

- 2 cans apple pie filling
- 1 box yellow cake mix
- 2 sticks of better, melted
- 1/2 cup caramel sauce
- 1/2 tsp cinnamon
- 1/2 cup chopped pecans

What to do:

1. Grease a 9x13 inch baking dish and preheat your oven to 350 degrees.
2. In the dish, stir together the apple pie filling, caramel sauce, and cinnamon. Spread evenly over the bottom of the dish.
3. Pour the dry cake mix over the mixture evenly.
4. Pour the melted butter on top of the dry cake mix.
5. Top with pecans.
6. Bake for 45 minutes or until the top is golden brown and apples are bubbly.
7. Serve with ice cream, if desired.

Halloween Peanut Butter Truffles

Makes 35-40

What you need:

- 16-oz Nutter Butter Cookies
- 8 oz cream cheese
- 8 oz Reese's Mini Peanut Butter Cups, quartered
- 12 oz milk chocolate chips
- 3/4 tbsp shortening
- Halloween colored sprinkles

What to do:

1. In a food processor, blend the Nutter Butters into fine crumbs.
2. Cube the cream cheese and place the cubes in the food processor and blend in with the Nutter Butter crumbs.
3. Transfer this mixture to a large bowl.
4. Fold the quartered Reese's cups into the mixture.
5. Roll the mixture into 1 inch balls and place on a sheet of parchment or wax paper on a baking sheet.
6. Freeze for about an hour.
7. Melt the chocolate chips and shortening in a microwave safe bowl in the microwave for 2-3 minutes, stirring every 30 seconds.
8. Dip the frozen balls into the melted chocolate.
9. Place the dipped balls back on the baking sheet to dry.
10. Add the sprinkles before the chocolate dries completely.

candy corn Blondies

Servings: 12

What you need:

- · 1 stick of butter
- · 1 large egg
- · 1 cup packed light brown sugar
- · 1 tbsp vanilla extract
- · 1 cup all-purpose flour
- · 2 cups candy corn, roughly chopped

What to do:

1. Preheat your oven to 350 degrees F and generously spray an 8x8 baking dish with cooking spray.
2. In a large bowl, melt the butter.
3. After a couple minutes, add the egg to the melted butter, followed by the brown sugar and vanilla. Whisk until smooth.
4. Stir in the flour until just combined.
5. Stir in the roughly chopped candy corn.
6. Pour the batter into the prepared pan and smooth out the top.
7. Bake for 22-25 minutes or until done. Cover for the last 5 minutes to prevent any exposed candy corn from burning.
8. Allow the blondies to cool before cutting into squares and serving.

Dirt Cake

Servings: 12

What you need:

- 1 package Oreos, crushed
- 1 8-oz package cream cheese, softened
- 1/2 cup butter, softened
- 1 cup powdered sugar
- 3 cups milk
- 1 12-oz container whipped cream
- 2 3.5-oz packages instant pudding (chocolate or vanilla)
- 2 tsp vanilla extract
- Gummy worms

What to do:

1. In a bowl, cream together the butter, cream cheese, powdered sugar, and vanilla.
2. In a separate large bowl, mix together the pudding mix and milk.
3. Fold the cream cheese mixture into the pudding mixture.
4. Add the whipped cream to the mixture.
5. Layer the crushed Oreos and the pudding mixture in small clear cups.
6. Add gummy worms to the top layer.

candy corn cheesecake

Servings: 6-8

What you need:

- 1 graham cracker crust
- 8 oz cream cheese, softened
- ¼ cup powdered sugar
- 2 tsp vanilla
- 1 cup sour cream
- 8 oz cool whip, thawed
- Yellow and orange food coloring
- Candy corn

What to do:

1. In a large mixing bowl, beat cream cheese until smooth then add powdered sugar and combine well.
2. Add the vanilla, sour cream, and whipped cream into the bowl and mix until everything is combined.
3. Divide the mixture evenly into three bowls.
4. Add yellow food coloring to one third and orange food coloring to another third. Leave the other third white.
5. Pour the yellow mixture onto the graham cracker crust.
6. Carefully pour the orange mixture onto the yellow mixture.
7. Carefully pour the white mixture onto the yellow mixture.
8. Sprinkle candy corn onto the top of the cheesecake.
9. Refrigerate for 2 hours before cutting and serving.

candy corn cookies

Servings: 8-10

What you need:

- 1 roll sugar cookie dough
- Candy corn

What to do:

1. Bake cookies according to directions on package.
2. When you remove them from the oven, let them cool for 2-3 minutes then place 3 or 4 candy corn pieces on each cookie.
3. Allow them to cool completely and serve.

Halloween Bundt Cake

Servings: 20

What you need:

- 1 15.25-oz white cake mix
- Ingredients listed on cake mix
- Orange, black, purple, and green food coloring
- 12 oz white frosting
- Halloween sprinkles

What to do:

1. Preheat oven to 325 degrees F and grease a bundt pan and set aside.
2. Mix the cake batter according to package directions.
3. Pour 1 cup of batter into a small bowl and stir in orange food coloring until well mixed.
4. Pour another cup of batter into a small bowl and stir in the purple food coloring. Repeat with the black.
5. Add green food coloring to the remaining batter and stir together well.
6. Pour the orange batter into the prepared pan then carefully pour the purple batter, followed by the black batter, then the green batter. Don't mix.
7. Bake according to package directions then let cool.
8. Divide the frosting evenly into 4 microwave safe bowls. Add one color of food coloring to each bowl and mix well.
9. One at a time, microwave the bowls of icing until fluid enough to drizzle over cake.
10. Drizzle the colors over the cake one at a time.
11. Let cool then apply sprinkles.

Halloween Cake Balls

Makes 4 dozen

What you need:

- 1 16-oz box yellow cake mix, plus ingredients the directions call for
- Orange, purple, and black candy melts (whichever you want, or use all)
- Halloween colored sprinkles
- Skewers

What to do:

1. Preheat your oven to 350 degrees F.
2. Combine all of the cake mix ingredients according to the box directions.
3. Place the cake batter in pastry bag or a large zip lock bag with the tip cut off.
4. Pipe the batter into a cake pop pan that has been sprayed with non-stick spray.
5. Bake for 18-20 minutes.
6. Let the cake pop pan rest for 5 minutes before opening it.
7. Place the cake pops onto a wire cooling rack to cool completely.
8. While pops are cooling, melt the candy melts according to package directions.
9. Insert the tip of a skewer into the melted candy, then into a cake pop. This helps it stick better.
10. Dip each cake pop into the melted candy and coat well.

11. Sprinkle each covered cake pop with sprinkles then let dry on wax paper.

Halloween Cookies

Servings: 10-12

What you need:

- 1 roll sugar cookies
- Black icing
- Orange icing
- White icing
- Green icing
- Cookie cutters (pumpkin, cat, ghost)

What to do:

1. Remove plastic from sugar cookie roll and let soften at room temperature.
2. Put parchment paper into a 13x9 inch baking dish. Extend the paper over the sides of the dish so you can easily lift the cookies out later.
3. Spray the parchment paper with non-stick spray.
4. Place the ball of dough in the dish and spread out into an even layer.
5. Bake according to package directions.
6. Remove them from the oven and let them cool for 5 minutes.
7. Remove the parchment paper from the pan.
8. Cut various Halloween shapes out of the cookie sheet. I used pumpkin, cat, and ghost.
9. When the shapes have cooled completely, spread icing on evenly. I put orange on the pumpkin shapes with black for the

face and green at the top, black for the cats with white facial features, and white for the ghosts with black facial features.

M&M Cookies

Makes 2 1/2 dozen

What you need:

- 2 ½ cups all-purpose flour
- 2 tsp cornstarch
- 3/4 tsp baking powder
- 1/2 tsp baking soda
- 1 cup butter
- 1 cup brown sugar
- 1/2 cup white sugar
- 1 large egg
- 2 tsp vanilla extract
- 1 11-oz bag Halloween M&M's

What to do:

1. Preheat your oven to 375 degrees and line 2 baking sheets with parchment paper.
2. In a mixing bowl, whisk together the flour, cornstarch, baking powder, baking soda, and salt. Set aside.
3. In a separate mixing bowl, mix together the butter and sugar with an electric mixer until creamy.
4. Mix in the egg and the additional egg yolk.
5. Mix in the vanilla.
6. Slowly mix in the flour mixture until combined.
7. Stir in the M&M's with a spoon, reserve 1/4 cup of M&M's for the tops of the cookies.

8. Scoop out 2 tbsp of dough at a time and form into a balls then place on the prepared baking sheet 2 inches apart.
9. Bake for 10-12 minutes until the edges are golden.
10. Allow the cookies to cool on the baking sheet for 5 minutes then transfer to a wire rack to cool completely.

Bloody Cheesecake

Servings: 16

What you need:

Crust:

- 8 chocolate graham crackers, finely crushed
- 5 tbsp melted butter

Cake:

- 3 8-oz blocks of cream cheese, at room temperature
- 3/4 cup sugar
- 1/3 cup unsweetened cocoa powder
- 4 large eggs, at room temperature
- 1 tsp vanilla
- 1/4 tsp salt
- 1/3 cup heavy whipping cream
- Red icing coloring or food coloring

Gel Frosting:

- 1/4 cup cold water
- 3 tsp cornstarch
- 1/4 cup light corn syrup
- 1 tsp vanilla
- Red icing coloring or food coloring

What to do:

1. Preheat your oven to 325 degrees F and line the bottom of a 9 inch spring form pan with parchment paper.
2. Combine the finely crushed graham crackers and the melted butter and press into the prepared pan.
3. In the bowl of a stand mixer (or with a hand mixer), beat the cream cheese and sugar until smooth. Add the cocoa powder and mix until combined, scraping down the sides as needed.
4. Add in the eggs, one at a time, mixing well between each addition.
5. Mix in the vanilla, salt, and heavy whipping cream and mix well.
6. Add red coloring until the mixture is a dark red color.
7. Pour the mixture into the prepared pan and spread out evenly.
8. Bake for 20 minutes at 325 degrees F then reduce the temperature to 225 degrees F and bake for another 30 minutes. Turn off the oven and leave the cheesecake in there, without opening the door, for 1 hour.
9. To make the gel frosting, stir together the water and cornstarch until no lumps remain. Pour it into a small saucepan and turn the heat to medium. Pour in the corn syrup and stir until it begins to thicken. Remove the mixture from the heat and stir in the vanilla and red coloring until the mixture is a deep red color.
10. Remove the cake from the oven and use a knife to loosen the edges from the sides of the pan then remove the whole cheesecake from the pan.
11. Once the gel frosting is cooled, pour it over the cheesecake.
12. Refrigerate for a few hours before serving.

Ghost Cookies

Servings: 10-12

What you need:

- 1 package white chocolate almond bark or candy melts
- 1 1-lb package Nutter Butter cookies
- About 4 tsp mini chocolate chips

What to do:

1. Melt almond bark or candy melts according to package directions.
2. Line two baking sheets with parchment paper.
3. Dip cookies, one at a time, into the melted almond bark/candy. Dip as much of the cookie as possible.
4. Lay dipped cookies flat on baking sheet.
5. Place two chocolate chips towards the top of the cookies to resemble eyes.
6. Let cool for 10-20 minutes.

Halloween Oreo Poke Cake

Servings: 8-10

What you need:

- Devil's Food cake mix, plus ingredients box calls for
- 5.1-oz box of vanilla instant pudding
- 1.5 cups milk
- 1 package of Oreos (the Halloween kind if you can find them)

What to do:

1. Spray a 9x13 inch baking dish with cooking spray and preheat your oven to 350 degrees F.
2. Prepare the Devil's Food cake according to box directions. Bake it according to the directions.
3. As soon as you get the cake out of the oven, poke holes all over it with the end of a wooden spoon. The more holes the better.
4. Whisk together the pudding mix and milk until no lumps remain. Pour the still liquid pudding mixture over the holes in the cake.
5. Put the Oreos in a large zip lock bag and crush them with a rolling pin or crush them in your food processor.
6. Spread the crumbled Oreos over the cake and pat down.
7. Cover and refrigerate for at least 2 hours.

Halloween Cake Batter Fudge

Servings: 8

What you need:

- 1 cup yellow cake mix
- 1 cup powdered sugar
- 1/2 stick of butter
- 1/4 cup milk
- 1/2 cup sprinkles

What to do:

1. Place all of the ingredients except the sprinkles in a microwave safe bowl and microwave for two minutes.
2. Remove from microwave and stir together well.
3. Stir in the sprinkles.
4. Pour into a greased square baking dish.
5. Cover and refrigerate for 2 hours.
6. Cut into squares once it's refrigerated.

Monster Cookies

Servings: 10-12

What you need:

- 1 tube sugar cookie dough
- 1 container vanilla icing
- Food coloring
- Candy eyeballs

What to do:

1. Bake cookies according to directions on package and let cool.
2. Divide icing into 4 or 5 small bowls.
3. Put a few drops of food coloring into each bowl (one color in each) and mix them together until well combined. I used yellow, orange, blue, and pink.
4. Ice the cookies with the different colors of icing. Use one color on each cookie.
5. Place a candy eyeball into the center of each cookie.

Witch's Brew Brownies

Servings: 16

(Made with leftover Halloween candy!)

What you need:

- 1 box brownie mix plus the ingredients the box calls for
- Leftover Halloween candy

What to do:

1. Mix the brownies according to box directions.
2. Before baking, top with whatever candy you are using. We used M&M's, mini Reese's cups, KitKat, and Twix).
3. Bake according to package directions.

frankenstein Brownies

Servings: 10-12

What you need:

- · 1 box brownie mix
- · Additional ingredients brownie mix calls for
- · 3 cups powdered sugar
- · 1 cup butter
- · 1 tsp vanilla extract
- · 1-2 tbsp whipping cream
- · Green food coloring
- · Black icing gel
- · Red icing gel
- · Candy corn

What to do:

1. Mix and bake brownies according to box directions and let cool.
2. In a large bowl, mix together the powdered sugar and butter until well blended.
3. Add vanilla and whipping cream until well blended.
4. Add green food coloring and mix and continue to add more until it's the color green you want it to be.
5. Cut brownies into rectangles.
6. Ice each brownie with green icing.
7. With the gel icing, draw Frankenstein's face and hair on each brownie. I drew a squiggly line for his hair in black, 2 dots of

red for eyes with tiny dots of black for pupils, a black dot for a nose, and a black mouth.

8. On the side of the brownies (the "neck" area) stick a candy corn in each side.

Halloween Rice Krispie Cake

Servings: 12-14

What you need:

- 3 tbsp butter
- 1 16-oz package mini marshmallows
- 6 cups Rice Krispies
- 1 cup candy corn
- 1 cup Reese's Pieces
- 2 tbsp almond bark, melted

What to do:

1. In a large saucepan, melt butter over low heat.
2. Add the marshmallows and stir until melted then remove from heat.
3. Stir in the Rice Krispies, candy corn and Reese's Pieces.
4. Pour the mixture into a greased bundt pan and press it firmly into the pan.
5. Let it cool.
6. Place a serving plate over the bundt pan and flip it all over so the cake is inverted onto the plate.
7. Drizzle melted almond bark onto the cake.
8. Slice and serve.

Spider Web Cupcakes

Servings: 10-12

What you need:

- 1 box white cake mix
- Cupcake liners (orange, white, or black)
- Additional ingredients cake mix calls for
- 1 container white icing
- 2-3 tubes black icing gel
- Black plastic spider rings

What to do:

1. Bake the cupcakes according to the directions on the box.
2. Let them cool then frost them with the white icing
3. With the black icing gel, draw a big circle on the cupcake.
4. Draw a medium circle in the big circle.
5. Draw a small circle in the medium circle.
6. Starting from the center circle, carefully drag a toothpick to the outer edge of the cupcake. I did 5 or 5 lines on each cupcake.
7. Carefully place a spider ring into the middle of each cupcake and push down.

Mummy Cookie Dough Truffles

Servings: 24

What you need:

- 1/2 cup butter, softened
- 3/4 cup packed brown sugar
- 1 tsp vanilla extract
- 1/2 tsp salt
- 2 cups flour
- 1 cup mini chocolate chips
- 1 can of sweetened condensed milk
- 12 oz of white chocolate chips
- Wilton candy eyes

What to do:

1. With a mixer, cream together the butter, brown sugar, vanilla, salt and sweetened condensed milk.
2. Add in the flour and mix until just combined.
3. Fold in the mini chocolate chips.
4. Place the dough in the refrigerator for 2 hours.
5. After it is chilled, roll the dough into tablespoon sized balls and place on parchment paper.
6. Melt the white chocolate chips in the microwave and dip each cookie dough ball into it to cover it completely.

7. Place the ball back on the parchment paper and drizzle a little bit of the melted chocolate chips over the ball then place 2 eyes on top.
8. Repeat with all of the cookie dough balls.

Mummy Ginger Truffles

Servings: 14

What you need:

- 40 gingersnap cookies
- 1/4 cup pumpkin puree
- 8 graham crackers
- 3 tbsp powdered sugar
- 1/4 tsp ground cinnamon
- 4 oz cream cheese, softened
- 2 1/2 cups white chocolate chips
- Red food coloring gel

What to do:

1. In the bowl of your food processor, add the gingersnap cookies and graham crackers and pulse until they are fine crumbs.
2. Add in the pumpkin puree, powdered sugar, cinnamon, salt, and cream cheese. Pulse until smooth.
3. Cover and freeze the mixture for about 30 minutes.
4. Roll the mixture into 14 balls.
5. Place a toothpick into each ball and freeze for about 20 minutes.
6. Melt the chocolate chips in a microwave safe bowl in the microwave.
7. Dip each ball into the melted chocolate then lay on a sheet of parchment paper.
8. Drizzle any leftover melted chocolate over the balls.

9. Dot two "mummy eyes" onto the balls with the red food coloring gel.

Ghost S'mores Brownies

Servings: 8-10

What you need:

Brownies:

- 3/4 cup unsweetened cocoa powder
- 1/2 tsp baking soda
- 2/3 cup butter, melted and divided in half
- 1/2 cup boiling water
- 2 cups sugar
- 2 large eggs
- 1 tsp vanilla extract
- 1/2 tsp salt
- 1 1/3 cup flour
- 2 cups chocolate chips

Ghost S'mores

- 1 stick of butter, melted
- 1 1/2 cups graham cracker crumbs
- 2 tbsp sugar
- A pinch of salt
- 1 package of ghost peeps
- Mini chocolate chips

What to do:

1. Preheat your oven to 350 degrees F and grease a 9x13 inch baking dish with nonstick spray and set aside.
2. Stir together 1 stick of melted butter, the graham cracker crumbs, 2 tbsp of sugar, and pinch of salt until mixed well. Press into the baking dish and bake for 10 minutes. Remove and set aside to cool.
3. In a mixing bowl, stir together the cocoa powder and baking soda then stir in 1/3 cup melted butter until smooth. Stir in the boiling water until the mixture is smooth.
4. Stir in the sugar and eggs and the rest of the butter. Mix well.
5. Stir in the vanilla and salt.
6. Pour in the flour and chocolate chips and stir until just combined.
7. Spread the batter into the baking dish over the graham cracker crust and bake for 35 minutes.
8. Place the ghost peeps on top of the brownie layer and broil for just a few seconds to a minute. Watch them carefully so they don't burn.
9. Place mini chocolate chips on the peeps to make eyes and a mouth.
10. Serve!

Butterfinger Cookies

Makes 2 1/2 dozen

What you need:

- · 1 3/4 cups all-purpose flour
- · 3/4 tsp baking soda
- · 1/4 tsp salt
- · 3/4 cup granulated sugar
- · 1/2 cup butter, softened
- · 1 large egg
- · 8 fun sized Butterfingers, chopped

What to do:

1. Preheat your oven to 350 degrees F.
2. In a mixing bowl, combine the flour, baking soda, and salt. Set aside.
3. In a separate mixing bowl, beat the sugar and butter with an electric mixer until creamy then mix in the egg.
4. Slowly mix in the flour mixture.
5. Stir in the Butterfinger pieces with a spoon.
6. Drop tablespoonful's of dough onto prepared baking sheet 2 inches apart.
7. Bake for 10-12 minutes or until lightly golden.
8. Allow the cookies to cool for 5 minutes then transfer them to a wire rack to cool completely.

Brain Cupcakes

Servings: 24

What you need:

- 1 box of yellow cake mix, plus ingredients box directions call for
- Cupcake tin liners
- White icing
- Red food coloring
- Piping bag

What to do:

1. Bake the cupcakes according to package directions then let cool completely.
2. While the cupcakes are cooling, mix together the white icing and 5-6 drops of red food coloring to make the icing a pinkish red color.
3. Ice all of the cupcakes normally then pipe 2 straight lines down the center of the cupcake, then pipe two squiggly lines on each side of the cupcake. It will look like a brain!

PARTY FOODS

Halloween Chicken and Rice Stuffed Peppers

Servings: 6-8

What you need:

- 2 chicken breasts
- 1 tsp cumin
- 1 tsp garlic powder
- 1 tsp chili powder
- 1 can of rotel tomatoes
- 4 orange bell peppers
- 2 cups Mexican rice
- 1 cup shredded cheddar cheese
- 1 can black beans, drained and rinsed

What to do:

1. Place the chicken in your crock pot with 1 tsp cumin, 1 tsp garlic powder, 1 tsp chili powder, and 1 can of rotel tomatoes. Cook on low for 8 hours or high for 4 hours. Remove from crock pot and shred.
2. In a mixing bowl, stir together the shredded chicken, rice, cheese, and black beans.
3. Cut the tops off of the 4 bell peppers. Remove the seeds. With a sharp knife, carefully cut triangle eyes, nose, and a mouth out of the pepper-- like a Jack O'Lantern.
4. Spoon the chicken and rice mixture into each pepper.
5. Bake at 350 degrees F for 30 minutes.

MUMMY HOT DOGS

Servings: 12

What you need:

- 1 package of hot dogs
- 1 package of refrigerated pizza crust

What to do:

1. Lay the uncooked pizza crust out and use a pizza cutter to cut it into long thin strips.
2. Cut the hotdogs into mummies. Starting at one end, cut up a couple inches to make the legs. About 2/3 of the way up, make slits on each side to make the arms.
3. Wrap the thin strips of pizza dough around the hotdog like it is the mummy's cloth.
4. Bake according to pizza crust directions.

Mummy Stuffed Jalapenos

Yield: 18

What you need:

- · 9 jalapeno peppers
- · 8 oz cream cheese
- · ½ cup shredded cheese
- · 3 tbsp ranch seasoning
- · 9 slices bacon, cut in half

What to do:

1. Preheat your oven to 375 degrees F.
2. Cut the jalapenos in half and remove the seeds.
3. In a microwave safe bowl, mix the cream cheese and shredded cheese and heat for 30 seconds then mix cheeses together.
4. Add ranch seasoning to cheeses and mix well.
5. Fill pepper halves with cheese mixture.
6. Cook bacon until almost done. It should still be pliable, not crispy and crumbly.
7. Pat excess grease from bacon and wrap around each pepper.
8. Place bacon wrapped peppers on a foil covered baking sheet and bake for 20 minutes.
9. Turn on the broiler and broil peppers for 2-3 minutes until the bacon looks crispy.
10. Remove from oven and cool slightly before serving.

Zombie Bacon

Servings: 4-6

What you need:

- 1 package bacon
- 1 cup brown sugar
- 1 tsp cayenne pepper

What to do:

1. Preheat your oven to 375 degrees F.
2. Line a large baking sheet with foil.
3. In a shallow bowl, mix together the brown sugar and cayenne pepper.
4. Dredge the bacon in the brown sugar mixture and lay each slice on the foil lined pan.
5. Bake for 15-20 minutes or until bacon is crisp.
6. Cool on a wire rack.

Mummy Pigs In A Blanket

Servings: 10-12

What you need:

- 2 cans breadstick dough
- 1 package hotdogs
- Capers

What to do:

1. Stretch breadstick dough until it's about a foot long.
2. Wrap dough around hot dogs. Make sure you let the hot dog show slightly through the dough.
3. Press capers in to make eyeballs.
4. Bake until bread is golden brown (whatever time the package says).

Graveyard Taco Dip

Servings: 10-12

What you need:

- 1 can of refried beans
- 2 cups of sour cream
- 1 package of taco seasoning
- 3 avocados, mashed
- 1 clove garlic, minced
- 1/2 small onion, diced small
- 1 cup salsa
- 1 cup of chopped green onions
- 2 large flour tortillas
- Tortilla chips or Fritos scoops

What to do:

1. Spread the refried beans evenly into the bottom deep serving dish (like Pyrex).
2. Mix together the sour cream and taco seasoning and spread it over the beans.
3. Mix together the mashed avocados, garlic, and onion and spread it over the sour cream mixture.
4. Spread the salsa over the avocado mixture.
5. Sprinkle the green onions over the salsa.
6. Cut ghost and tombstone shapes out of the tortillas and bake them at 350 degrees F for 10 minutes or until hard. Place the shapes into the dip before serving.
7. Serve with chips.

Zombie Dip (Guacamole)

Servings: 8-10

What you need:

- · 2 roma tomatoes
- · 1 jalapeno
- · 1 small onion
- · 4 avocados
- · 2 lemons
- · Salt to taste

What to do:

1. Chop the tomatoes and onion and combine.
2. Cut the stem off the jalapeno and cut it in half. Remove the seeds and stems. Chop and add it to the onion and tomato.
3. Cut open, remove skins and seeds, and roughly chop the avocados. Add them to the mixture.
4. Use a masher (or your clean hands) to mash up the avocados and to combine the mixture.
5. Squeeze in the lemon juice (watch for seeds.)
6. Add salt to taste.

Mini Zombie Brains
(Meatballs)

Servings: 8-10

What you need:

- Large pack of frozen meatballs
- 1 16 oz bottle of barbeque sauce
- 1 16 oz jar of chili sauce

What to do:

1. Combine barbeque and chili sauce in a small sauce pan over medium heat until mixed well.
2. Put all the meatballs in a crock pot and pour the sauce mixture on top. Stir until all meatballs are coated.
3. Cook them on high for 4-5 hours, stirring every hour or so.
4. Serve while they are still hot.

Spider Deviled Eggs

Servings: 12

What you need:

- · 6 boiled eggs
- · 3 tbsp mayonnaise
- · 2 tsp spicy mustard
- · Salt and pepper, to taste
- · Whole, pitted black olives

What to do:

1. Peel the eggs and cut them in half lengthwise.
2. Scoop out the yolks and mash together in a bowl.
3. Stir in the mayonnaise, mustard, salt and pepper.
4. Lay the egg whites on a serving tray and scoop the egg yolk mixture onto them.
5. Cut 6 olives in half lengthwise. Place one olive half on each egg yolk mixture as the spider's body.
6. Thinly slice more olives to make the spider legs. Place 4 legs on each side of the spider's body.

Pumpkin Deviled Eggs

Servings: 8-10

What you need:

- 6 eggs, boiled, cooled, peeled
- 2 tbsp mayonnaise
- 2 tsp tomato paste
- 1 tsp ketchup
- 1/2 tsp paprika plus more to sprinkle
- 1/2 tsp spicy brown mustard
- 1/4 tsp Sriracha
- Salt to taste
- 1 green onion

What to do:

1. Slice the eggs lengthwise and gently remove the yolks.
2. Place yolks, mayonnaise, tomato paste, ketchup, paprika, spicy brown mustard, Sriracha, and salt in a bowl and mash until very smooth.
3. Spoon the mixture back into the egg white and pat the surface to make the yolks look smooth and round.
4. Use a toothpick to make indentions in the yolks to look like the lines of a pumpkin.
5. Sprinkle with paprika.
6. Cut the onion to look like tiny pumpkin stems and place one stem at the top of each yolk.

cocktail Fingers

Servings: 10-12

What you need:

- 2 14-oz packages little smokies
- 1 24-oz bottle Bull's Eye BBQ sauce
- 8 oz grape jelly
- 4 oz juice from jar of jalapenos

What to do:

1. Turn your crock pot on low.
2. Place BBQ sauce, jelly, and jalapeno juice in crockpot and whisk together until combined.
3. Add in little smokies and mix with sauce.
4. Cover and cook for approximately 4 hours, stirring every half hour.
5. Serve with toothpicks.

Cheesy Breadstick Bones

Makes 10 breadsticks

What you need:

- · 1 lb homemade or store-bought pizza dough
- · 1 stick of butter, melted
- · 1 cup grated Parmesan cheese
- · 1 cup shredded mozzarella cheese
- · Marinara sauce, for serving

What to do:

1. Preheat your oven to 375 degrees F and line two baking sheets with parchment paper.
2. Divide the dough into 10 balls then roll each ball into an (approx.) 8 inch rope that is slightly thicker on the ends.
3. Place 5 breadsticks on each baking sheet spaced about 2 inches apart.
4. Use scissors to cut a 1 inch slit on the end of each breadstick and stretch them apart to make them look like the ends of bones.
5. Brush the breadsticks with the melted butter and sprinkle with the grated parmesan cheese.
6. Bake for 15 minutes then remove from the oven and top with mozzarella and bake for another 5 minutes.
7. Remove from the oven and serve with marinara sauce for dipping.

Bloody Beet Chips

Servings: 1-2

What you need:

- 3-4 medium sized beets
- 1 tbsp coconut oil
- Sea salt, to taste

What to do:

1. Preheat your oven to 200 degrees F.
2. Thinly slice the beets using a mandolin or the slicer of a food processor.
3. Lay the beet slices in a single layer on a baking pan (or two baking pans) lined with parchment paper.
4. Melt the coconut oil and brush it onto the beets.
5. Bake the beets for 2 hours. Turn them over every 30 minutes.
6. Take them out of the oven and let them sit for 5-10 minutes.
7. Sprinkle beets with salt before serving.

OTHER TREATS

BIack Candy AppIes

Servings: 6

What you need:

- 2 cups granulated sugar
- 3/4 cup water
- 1/2 cup light corn syrup
- Several drops of black gel food coloring
- 6 Granny Smith apples
- Bamboo skewers
- Candy thermometer

What to do:

1. Place a sheet of parchment paper over a large baking sheet.
2. Insert bamboo skewers into apples and set aside.
3. In a medium saucepan, combine the sugar, water, corn syrup, and food coloring. Stir constantly over medium heat until sugar has dissolved and the mixture is smooth. Allow it to boil until it reaches 310 degrees F.
4. Carefully dip the apples into the sugar mixture and set on the parchment paper for an hour or two until cooled.

Apple Sandwich with Teeth

Servings: 1-2

What you need:

- 1 honey crisp apple
- 2 tbsp peanut butter
- Marshmallows
- A drizzle of honey

What to do:

1. Core the apple.
2. Slice the apple into ½ inch slices.
3. Put peanut butter onto each slice of apple.
4. Place 5-6 marshmallows on each apple as teeth.
5. Add honey and top with another slice of apple.

Peanut Butter Pie

Servings: 6-8

What you need:

- 1 package Halloween Oreos
- 4 tbsp butter, melted
- 1 cup peanut butter
- 8 oz cream cheese, softened
- 1 cup powdered sugar
- 8 oz cool whip, thawed

What to do:

1. Preheat your oven to 350 degrees F.
2. Place Oreos into a food processor and pulse until they're fine crumbs.
3. Add the melted butter to the Oreo crumbs and stir with a fork to combine.
4. Press into a pie pan and bake for 7 minutes or until set. Then allow to cool completely.
5. In a large mixing bowl, combine peanut butter and cream cheese and beat until smoothed together.
6. Add the powdered sugar and beat until combined.
7. Add the cool whip and mix until combined.
8. Pour into the crust and smooth the top.
9. Chill for at least 2 hours before serving.

Bone Rice Krispie Treats

Servings: 12

What you need:

- 1/4 cup butter
- 1 10-oz package of large marshmallows
- 6 cups Rice Krispies
- 1 cup white chocolate chips

What to do:

1. In a large saucepan over medium heat, melt the butter and stir in the marshmallows until they are melted.
2. Turn the heat off and stir the Rice Krispies into the melted marshmallows.
3. Coat a 9x13 inch baking dish with non-stick spray.
4. Pour the cereal/marshmallow mixture into the pan.
5. Put a sheet of wax or parchment paper over the top of the mixture and press the mixture down firmly.
6. Use your hands to form rice krispie treats into a bone shape. If you can find a bone shaped cookie cutter that will work even better.
7. Lay the bones on a sheet of parchment paper until they have firmed up.
8. Heat the white chocolate chips until melted.
9. Dip the front side (the one that faces up) of each bone into the melted chocolate.
10. Lay back on the parchment paper to dry.

BOWl Of WORMS

Servings: 5-7

What you need:

- · 2 3-oz packages of red Jello
- · 1 package of unflavored gelatin
- · 3/4 cup whipping cream
- · 3 cups water
- · 15 drops green food coloring
- · 100 flexible straws
- · 1 tall container, like a 1 liter empty carton

What to do:

1. This one can get very messy but it is very neat! First, go ahead and prepare your "worm making gadget". Pull out the flexible part of each straw and make it straight. Gather the straws and place them all into the carton. You want a tight fit. If it isn't a tight fit, secure the straws with a rubber band.
2. Boil the water then stir in the Jello mix and the gelatin and stir for 2 minutes.
3. Stir in the whipping cream and green food coloring. This makes the worms not be so see-through and red.
4. Pour the mixture into the straws and refrigerate for 4-6 hours.
5. To get the worms out of the straws hold the straws under warm water and they will slide right out. Drain off all the water then serve!

Brain Rice Krispie Treats

Servings: 16

What you need:

- 3 tbsp butter
- 10 oz bag of mini marshmallows
- Red food coloring
- 6 cups Rice Krispie cereal
- Red gel icing

What to do:

1. Melt the butter in a pot over medium heat.
2. Add in the marshmallows and heat until melted, stirring constantly.
3. Add in several drops of red food coloring to make it the color of a brain.
4. Add in the cereal and stir until it is coated evenly with the marshmallow mixture.
5. While the mixture is still warm (but not hot) scoop up a handful and shape it into a brain shape and then press a knife down the middle to make an indention.
6. Place each brain on a sheet of wax paper and let them cool/harden.
7. After they're cooled, drizzle with red gel.

candY Apple Bar

Servings: 12

What you need:

· 12 apples
· 1 jar of caramel
· 2 tbsp milk
· Bamboo skewers
· Various toppings (crushed Oreos, crushed toffee pieces, nuts, marshmallows, chocolate chips)

What to do:

1. Core each apple and cut into 6 slices.
2. Place each slice on a bamboo skewer and arrange on a serving tray.
3. Pour the caramel into a microwave safe bowl and add the milk. Stir together then microwave for 30 seconds or until warm. Stir again. Place next to or on the apple serving tray.
4. Place the various toppings in small bowls and arrange around the apple serving tray.
5. To enjoy, dip each apple into caramel then into desired toppings.

candy corn Bark

Servings: 8-10

What you need:

- 1 bag waffle style pretzels
- 1 16-oz package white almond bark
- 1 11-oz package caramel bits
- 1 9-oz bag candy corn

What to do:

1. Line a baking sheet with parchment paper and put the pretzels on the baking sheet in an even layer.
2. Melt caramel according to package directions and spoon half of it onto pretzels then allow them to cool for 5 minutes.
3. Melt almond bark according to package directions and pour over the caramel and spread evenly.
4. Allow the almond bark to cool for 5 minutes then pour on the rest of the caramel.
5. Allow it to cool for a minute then add the candy corn to the top.
6. Allow the bark to harden and then cut it into pieces.

candy corn cream Ball

Servings: 10-12

What you need:

- 8 oz cream cheese, softened
- 8 oz marshmallow cream
- 1/2 cup white chocolate chips
- 1.5 cups candy corn, chopped
- Vanilla wafers, animal crackers, or graham crackers

What to do:

1. In a large bowl, combine cream cheese, marshmallow cream with a mixer.
2. Fold in white chocolate chips.
3. Place mixture in freezer for 30 minutes.
4. Remove mixture from freezer and spoon out onto a large piece of parchment paper.
5. Wrap parchment paper around the mixture and form into a ball shape.
6. Put it back in the freezer for about 30 minutes.
7. Pour the chopped candy corn onto a plate and roll the hardened ball mixture around in them until it is coated.
8. Serve with vanilla wafers, animal crackers, graham crackers, etc.

candY corn crunch

Servings: 10-12

What you need:

- 1 bag popcorn, popped
- 2 cups pretzels, broken into small pieces
- 1 bag orange candy melts
- Halloween sprinkles
- 1 small bag candy corn

What to do:

1. Place popcorn and pretzels in a large bowl.
2. Melt the candy melts according to the package directions.
3. Pour melted candy over the popcorn and pretzels and stir until coated.
4. Add sprinkles and candy corn and mix to blend everything together.
5. Spread out on a large piece of parchment paper in an even layer and allow it to dry.
6. After it's dried, place it in a serving bowl or store in an air tight container.

candy corn Marshmallow People

Servings: 14-16

What you need:

- 1 bag of jumbo marshmallows
- 1 package almond bark or candy melts
- Vegetable oil
- Yellow food coloring
- Orange food coloring
- Black icing gel

What to do:

1. Melt almond bark/candy melts according to package directions.
2. Divide the melted almond bark/candy melts in half.
3. Add orange food coloring to one half and yellow food coloring to the other half.
4. Dip the marshmallows about halfway into the orange chocolate and set on a piece of parchment paper to dry.
5. Once all marshmallows are dried (it won't take long), dip them about a quarter of the way into the yellow chocolate and set back on the parchment paper to dry.

6. Using a very small amount of the black icing gel for each, carefully make two eyes on the marshmallows and allow them to dry.

caramel Apple cream cheese spread

Servings: 8

What you need:

- · 8 oz cream cheese, at room temperature
- · 8 oz caramel sauce
- · 1 cup toffee bits
- · Sliced apples

What to do:

1. Place the cream cheese on a serving dish.
2. Pour the caramel over the cream cheese. You can use more or less, just depending on your preference.
3. Sprinkle with toffee bits.
4. Serve with sliced apples.

Caramel Apple Fruit Pizza

Servings: 10-12

What you need:

- 1 roll of sugar cookie dough
- 8-oz cream cheese, softened
- 2 cups powdered sugar
- 2 cups cool whip
- 4 apples; cored, and sliced thinly

What to do:

1. Roll the sugar cookie dough out onto a large round cookie sheet. Roll it into a ball and flatten it out into a circle like a pizza crust.
2. Bake according to package directions then set aside to let cool completely.
3. In a bowl with a mixer, mix the cream cheese for a few seconds until it is light and fluffy. Add in the powdered sugar and cool whip and mix until combined and fluffy.
4. Once the cookie crust is cooled, spread the cream cheese mixture over it evenly.
5. Lay the apples over the topping.
6. Cut into "pizza" slices and serve immediately or refrigerate.

Cheese and Pretzel Broomsticks

Servings: 12-14

What you need:

- 6 sticks of string cheese
- 1 cup pretzel sticks
- 18-20 chive sprigs

What to do:

1. Unwrap the sting cheeses and cut each into thirds.
2. Spread out the end of the string cheese pieces to resemble bristles of a broom.
3. Stick a pretzel stick into non-bristled end of the cheese.
4. Tie a chive sprig around the top of the broom head, right under where you stuck the pretzel in.

Chocolate covered pretzels

Servings: 12-14

What you need:

- 1 bag of pretzels (any kind/shape/size)
- 1 package almond bark (chocolate or white chocolate)
- Sprinkles (white, orange, black, and/or yellow)
- Halloween themed candy

What to do:

1. Melt the almond bark over a double broiler.
2. Dip the pretzels into the melted chocolate and lay in an even layer on parchment paper or evenly lay pretzels on parchment paper then drizzle the chocolate over the pretzels.
3. Sprinkle the sprinkles over the pretzels before the chocolate is completely dried.
4. Stick candy to the chocolate before it is completely dried. You can really be creative with the decoration of these chocolate covered pretzels.

Chocolate Turtle Apple Slices

Servings: 2

What you need:

- 2 large Fuji apples
- 4 cups chocolate chips
- 1 cup caramels, melted
- Chopped pecans
- Popsicle sticks

What to do:

1. Slice the apples into half inch thick pieces lengthwise.
2. Make a slit into the bottom of each apple and insert a popsicle stick.
3. Melt the chocolate chips then dip each apple slice into the melted chocolate to completely cover it.
4. Place the covered apple slice on a sheet of parchment paper.
5. Melt the caramel and drizzle it over the apple slices.
6. Sprinkle chopped pecans over the apples.
7. Refrigerate for 1 hour then serve immediately.

CRescen+ ROll Wi+ch Ha+S

Servings: 8

What you need:

- 1 package crescent rolls
- Salami, cut into strips
- 4 oz cheddar cheese, cut into strips
- 4 oz cheddar cheese cut into cubes
- 4 oz Swiss cheese, cut into strips

What to do:

1. Open the crescent rolls and separate them and lay them out.
2. Place a strip of salami, a strip of cheddar, and a strip of Swiss onto the wide part of each crescent roll.
3. Roll up the wide part of the roll, creating a hat brim, leave the rest of the roll unrolled so that it looks like a witch's hat.
4. Place extra strips of Swiss cheese above the brim and place a cube of cheddar in the center of the Swiss cheese. This makes a hat band and buckle.
5. Bake according to crescent roll package directions.

Ghost Pancakes

Servings: 4-6

What you need:

- Your favorite pancake batter
- Chocolate chips

What to do:

1. Hit a greased griddle on medium high heat.
2. Spoon the pancake batter into oddly shaped blobs onto the griddle. The shape doesn't matter too much as long as they aren't round. Whatever shape you think ghosts are.
3. Place two chocolate chips on the pancakes for eyes and another for the mouth.
4. When the batter begins to bubble, flip the pancake and cook for another 30 seconds-1 minute.
5. Remove from the pan and serve.

Ghost Strawberries

Servings: 12

What you need:

- 12 strawberries
- 12 oz white chocolate chips
- 1/4 cup mini chocolate chips

What to do:

1. Wash and dry the strawberries.
2. Melt the white chocolate chips
3. Dip each strawberry into the white chocolate to cover it up to the stem and lay on parchment paper.
4. Place mini chocolate chips on the strawberry to make eyes and a mouth.

Halloween Apple Mouth Bites

Servings: 1-2

What you need:

- · 1 apple
- · 1 cup mini marshmallows
- · ½ cup peanut butter

What to do:

1. Slice the apple into ¼ inch slices.
2. Generously spread peanut butter on one side of each apple slice.
3. Stick marshmallows in the peanut butter on the apple and top with another slice of apple.

Halloween Caramel Apples

Servings: 6

What you need:

- 6 wooden skewers
- 6 Gala apples
- 14 oz package caramels
- 2 tbsp milk
- Halloween sprinkles
- Candy Corn

What to do:

1. Insert skewers into apples and set aside.
2. Combine caramels and milk in a microwave safe bowl and heat on high for 2 minutes. Stir every 30 seconds.
3. Roll each apple in caramel, turning to coat well.
4. Allow apples to dry on parchment paper.
5. When apples are almost dry, roll them in candy corn and Halloween sprinkles.

Halloween Marshmallow Pops

Servings: varies – use whatever amount of ingredients you want to make as many as you want!

What you need:

- Marshmallows
- Black or orange candy melts
- Halloween sprinkles
- Cake pop sticks

What to do:

1. Skewer each marshmallow onto a cake pop stick.
2. Melt the candy melts.
3. Dip each marshmallow in melted candy then apply sprinkles.

Halloween S'mores

Servings: 15

What you need:

- 15 graham cracker rectangles
- 15 jumbo marshmallows
- 30 small rectangles of Hershey's chocolate
- Sprinkles (yellow, orange, black)

What to do:

1. Break each graham cracker into squares.
2. Place 15 squares on a large microwave safe plate. If 15 won't fit, do this in smaller batches.
3. Place 2 rectangles of chocolate on each graham cracker and microwave for 10 seconds.
4. Place 1 jumbo marshmallow on each graham cracker and chocolate in the microwave and heat for an additional 10-15 seconds.
5. Top each s'more with another graham cracker square.
6. Pour sprinkles onto a plate and carefully roll the edges of each s'more in the sprinkles.
7. Serve immediately.

Halloween Sweet Popcorn

Servings: 8-10

What you need:

- 1 bag popcorn, popped
- 1 package vanilla candy melts
- ¾ cup candy corn
- Halloween colored candy corn

What to do:

1. Place popped popcorn in a large bowl.
2. Melt candy melts according to package directions and pour it on top of the popcorn.
3. Add in the candy corn and stir until well combined.
4. Pour mixture onto a baking sheet covered with parchment paper.
5. Add sprinkles on top of mixture.
6. Allow the mixture to harden and store in zip lock bag if not serving immediately.

Halloween Trail Mix

Servings: 20

What you need:

- 1 bag of pretzels
- 1 bag of bugles
- 1 small box of Captain Crunch cereal
- 1 bag of candy corn
- 2 cups of Reese's Pieces Muddy Buddies (or store bought)
- 1 cup white chocolate chips

What to do:

1. Mix all of the ingredients together in a large bowl.
2. Serve at a party or place in individual bags!

Jack O' Lantern Cuties

Servings: varies

What you need:

- Cuties, mandarin oranges, or tangerines
- Sharpie marker

What to do:

1. This is really simple but a great idea. Draw Jack O'Lantern eyes, nose, and mouth on cuties with a black permanent marker. The kids will love it!

Melted Witch Pudding Parfaits

Servings: 6

What you need:

- · 1 box pistachio pudding mix
- · 1.5 cups cold milk
- · Brownies, crumbled into small pieces
- · Oreos, crushed
- · Whipped cream
- · Halloween sprinkles
- · Paper straws, cut in half
- · Black construction paper
- · Clear plastic cups

What to do:

1. Mix together the pistachio pudding mix and milk and refrigerate until set.
2. While the pudding is setting, begin layering the parfaits. First add brownie pieces to the bottom of each cup. Next, add a layer of whipped cream, then a layer of crushed Oreos. Next, add the pistachio pudding then the sprinkles.
3. Cut witches shoes out of the construction paper and tape or paste it to the end of each half straw.
4. Place two half straws with feet up into each parfait.

Melted Witches

Servings: 8

What you need:

- Green candy melts, a little over a cup
- 1/2 cup mini chocolate chips
- 8 small pretzel sticks
- 8 mini Reese's peanut butter cups
- 8 Halloween Oreos
- 8 Hershey's hugs

What to do:

1. Lay out a sheet of parchment paper on a large cookie sheet.
2. Make broomsticks with the pretzels and mini Reese's cups. Just push a pretzel into a Reese's cup.
3. .Count out and separate 16 mini chocolate chips for the eyes.
4. Melt the green candy melts in a pot over low heat. Once it is melted, dot a little bit onto the center of each Oreo then stick a Hershey's hug onto the dot of melted candy to make the witch's hat.
5. Have the broomsticks, hats, and eyes set out so you can work quickly before the candy dries.
6. Spoon the remaining melted candy onto the parchment paper into circles about 3-4 inches in diameter.
7. As soon as you get the candy onto the parchment paper, quickly melt the chocolate chips (except for the 16 you set aside for the eyes) then drizzle a small amount onto the green

circles and swirl around with a toothpick to give it a marbled look.

8. Add 2 mini chocolate chips to each circle for the eyes, add the hats, and lay the broomsticks across each circle.

Melted Jack O'Lantern Brownies

Makes 12 brownies

What you need:

Brownies:

- · 3/4 cup unsweetened cocoa powder
- · 1/2 tsp baking soda
- · 2/3 cup butter, melted and divided in half
- · 1/2 cup boiling water
- · 2 cups sugar
- · 2 large eggs
- · 1 tsp vanilla extract
- · 1/2 tsp salt
- · 1 1/3 cup flour
- · 2 cups chocolate chips

Melted Jack O'Lanterns

- · 12-oz orange candy melts
- · 12 large marshmallows
- · 1/2 cup mini chocolate chips

What to do:

1. Preheat your oven to 350 degrees F and grease a 9x13 inch baking dish with nonstick spray and set aside.

2. In a mixing bowl, stir together the cocoa powder and baking soda then stir in 1/3 cup melted butter until smooth. Stir in the boiling water until the mixture is smooth.
3. Stir in the sugar and eggs and the rest of the butter. Mix well.
4. Stir in the vanilla and salt.
5. Pour in the flour and chocolate chips and stir until just combined.
6. Spread the batter into the baking dish and bake for 35 minutes.
7. Remove from the oven and set aside to cool.
8. Once cooled, slice the brownies into 12 even squares and set on a sheet of parchment paper a few inches apart from each other.
9. Melt the candy melts according to package directions and using a fork or toothpicks, dip a marshmallow into the melted candy and without shaking off the excess, quickly set it on top of a brownie. You want some of the excess melted candy to drip off onto the brownie. If there isn't enough excess, spoon a small amount onto the top of the marshmallow or around the marshmallow on brownie. Before the candy coating is completely dried, place a chocolate chip on top of the marshmallow for a stem and then place two chocolate chips on the front of the marshmallow for eyes. Repeat this whole process with the remaining marshmallows.
10. Once you have finished the eyes and stems on all the Jack O'Lanterns, melt the remaining chocolate chips for 20-30 seconds until melted and smooth. Dip the end of a toothpick into the chocolate and "draw" a chocolate Jack O'Lantern mouth onto each marshmallow.

oreo Butter

Servings: 20

What you need:

- 1 package or Oreos
- 1/4 cup of refined* coconut oil, melted

What to do:

1. Place the Oreos and coconut oil in a food processor.
2. Let the food processor run for 5 minutes, scraping down the sides every minute or two.
3. Store in an airtight container at room temperature.

*refined coconut oil doesn't have a coconut taste to it

Oreo Rice Krispie Treats

Servings: 10-12

What you need:

- 3 tbsp butter
- 4 cups mini marshmallows
- 6 cups Rice Krispies cereal
- 15 Halloween Oreos, crushed

What to do:

1. Melt the butter over low heat in a large saucepan.
2. Add marshmallows and stir completely until they are all melted then remove the heat.
3. Pour Rice Krispies and Oreos into a large bowl and mix together.
4. Spray some cooking spray onto a spatula and add marshmallows to the bowl with rice Krispies and Oreos and stir until combined.
5. Gently press mixture into a 13 x 9 inch pan that is coated with cooking spray.
6. Let them cool then cut into squares.

Owl Pretzels

Servings: 10-12

What you need:

- 1 bag large pretzels
- White chocolate almond bark or candy melts
- Mini Oreos
- Black sprinkles
- Black icing gel
- Black licorice
- Chocolate chips

What to do:

1. Melt almond bark/candy melts according to package directions.
2. Dip large pretzel into the melted almond bark and place on baking sheet lined with parchment paper.
3. Lightly sprinkle the sprinkles onto the covered pretzel.
4. Separate the mini Oreos and place one half on each top rounded part on each pretzel.
5. Drop a small round blob of the melted almond bark/candy melt onto the center of each Oreo and place a chocolate chip on each blob.
6. Draw a beak with the black icing gel between the two Oreo eyes (slightly lower).
7. Draw feet onto the bottom of the pretzel with the black icing gel.
8. Cut the black licorice into small pieces and use as eyebrows.

peanut Butter and Jelly Spiders

Servings: 1

What you need:

· 2 slices of bread
· Peanut butter
· Jelly
· 2 raisins or chocolate chips
· 8 pretzel sticks

What to do:

1. Spread the peanut butter and jelly onto a slice of bread and lay the other slice of bread on top.
2. Using a large cookie cutter (or just a knife) cut the majority of the center of the sandwich out into a circle.
3. Stick 4 pretzel sticks into each side for the legs and 2 raisins or chocolate chips on the top for eyes.

peanut Butter Monster Energy Balls

Servings: 8-10

What you need:

- 2 cups oatmeal
- 1/2 cup shelled sunflower seeds
- 1/4 cup flaxseed
- 1 cup raisins
- 1 tsp cinnamon
- 1/2 tsp nutmeg
- 1 cup peanut butter
- 1/2 cup honey
- Candy Eyes

What to do:

1. Combine the oatmeal, sunflower seeds, flaxseed, raisins, cinnamon, and nutmeg in a large bowl.
2. In a smaller bowl, stir together the honey and the peanut butter.
3. Add the peanut butter mixture to the oatmeal mixture and mix together well.
4. Shape into 1 inch balls. (I wore plastic gloves to prevent making a huge sticky mess.)
5. Place 1 or 2 eyes on each ball.
6. Serve or store covered in the refrigerator.

peanut Butter Spider cookies

Makes 48 cookies

What you need:

- 1/2 cup butter, at room temperature
- 1/2 cup peanut butter
- 1/2 cup brown sugar
- 1/2 cup granulated sugar
- 1 egg
- 2 tbsp milk
- 1 tsp vanilla
- 1 3/4 cup flour
- 1 tsp baking soda
- 1/2 tsp salt
- 48 mini Reese's cups, unwrapped and frozen
- 96 Melton candy eyes
- 1/2 cup chocolate chips

What to do:

1. Preheat oven to 375 degrees F.
2. In a mixing bowl, beat together the butter, peanut butter, egg, brown sugar, granulated sugar, vanilla, and milk.
3. In a medium bowl, whisk together the flour, baking soda, and salt.
4. Slowly add the flour mixture to the wet mixture and beat until just combined.

5. Form into 1" balls and place on a greased cookie sheet 2 inches apart. Bake for 10-12 minutes or until golden.
6. While the cookies are still warm, gently press an upside down frozen mini Reese's cup on top of each cookie. Place two candy eyes on the front of each Reese's cup.
7. Place the chocolate chips in the bottom of a ziplock bag and microwave for 20 seconds or until melted.
8. Clip a VERY small piece off the corner of the bag and pipe 8 "legs" around the Reese's cup.
9. Refrigerate for 10 minutes to allow legs to set.

popcorn Balls

Servings: 4-6

What you need:

- 1 bag popcorn, popped
- ¼ cup butter
- 1 10-oz bag mini marshmallows
- ½ tsp vanilla extract
- 1 cup Reese's Pieces

What to do:

1. Melt butter in a large saucepan.
2. Add marshmallows and stir until they are melted then remove from heat and stir in vanilla.
3. Add popcorn to the marshmallow mixture and mix together.
4. Gently fold in Reese's Pieces.
5. When mixture has cooled enough to handle, scoop about 1 cup of popcorn mixture and form it into a ball with your hands. I sprayed my hands with cooking spray so everything wouldn't stick to my hands.
6. Place each ball on a baking sheet lined with parchment paper and allow them to cool.

Pumpkin & Chocolate Strawberries

Servings: 8-10

What you need:

- 1 pint strawberries, washed and dried
- 1 package white chocolate almond bark or candy melts
- Orange food dye

What to do:

1. Melt almond bark or candy melts according to package directions.
2. Once it's melted, stir in orange food dye. Use enough to where its bright orange like a pumpkin.
3. Completely dip the strawberries into the melted chocolate. You should still be able to see the leaves but you shouldn't be able to see anymore red from the strawberry.
4. Lay strawberries on a sheet of parchment paper and gently draw vertical "pumpkin lines" down the chocolate.
5. Refrigerate strawberries until the chocolate is completely dried.

Pumpkin Cheese Ball

Servings: 10

What you need:

- 2 8-oz blocks of cream cheese, softened
- 2 tbsp hidden valley ranch mix
- 3 green onions, diced
- 1 orange bell pepper, diced, save the stem
- 2 cups shredded cheddar cheese
- 4 large rubber bands
- Crackers

What to do:

1. Using an electric mixer, whip together the 2 blocks of cream cheese.
2. Mix in the ranch seasoning.
3. Mix in the green onions and diced pepper.
4. Stir in 1 cup of the shredded cheddar.
5. Using your hands, form the cream cheese mixture into somewhat of a ball. It doesn't have to be perfect.
6. Spread out a large sheet of saran wrap.
7. Sprinkle a handful of cheese on the saran wrap then top the shredded cheese with the cream cheese mixture.
8. Press the rest of the shredded cheese onto the outside of the cheese ball.
9. Wrap the shredded cheese covered cheese ball in the sheet of saran wrap. Wrap the whole thing in another large sheet of saran wrap. Wrap it tightly.

10. Double wrap 4 rubber bands around the cheeseball to make indentions like a pumpkin has.
11. Refrigerate for 2 hours then remove the rubber bands and saran wrap.
12. Place the stem of the bell pepper into the center of the cheeseball to look like a pumpkin stem.
13. Serve with crackers.

Pumpkin Cinnamon Roll Casserole

Servings: 4-6

What you need:

- 2 tbsp butter, melted
- 2 12-oz cans of refrigerated cinnamon rolls with icing
- 4 eggs
- 1/2 cup heavy whipping cream
- 2 tsp cinnamon
- 2 tsp vanilla
- 2 tsp pumpkin pie spice
- 1 cup chopped pecans
- 1/4 cup maple syrup

What to do:

1. Heat your oven to 375 degrees F.
2. Pour the melted butter into a greased 9x13 inch baking dish.
3. Separate both cans of dough, set icing aside, and cut each roll into 6 pieces.
4. Place the cinnamon roll pieces in the baking dish.
5. In a medium bowl, whisk together the eggs, whipping cream, cinnamon, pumpkin pie spice and vanilla.
6. Evenly pour the egg mixture over the cinnamon rolls.
7. Sprinkle the pecans over the casserole.
8. Drizzle the maple syrup over the casserole.
9. Bake for 25 minutes or until the casserole is golden brown.

10. Remove from the oven and let cool for 5-10 minutes.
11. Remove the lid from the icing containers and microwave them for 15-20 seconds or until they are thinned out.
12. Drizzle the icing over the casserole and serve.

Pumpkin Crisp

Servings: 8

What you need:

- 1 15-oz can pumpkin
- 3/4 cup evaporated milk
- 1 cup sugar
- 1 tsp vanilla
- 1/2 tsp cinnamon
- 1/4 tsp nutmeg
- 1 yellow cake mix
- 1 cup pecans
- 1/2 cup butter, melted

What to do:

1. Stir together the first six ingredients and pour into lightly greased pan.
2. Sprinkle dry cake mix evenly over pumpkin mixture.
3. Top with pecans and drizzle with the melted butter.
4. Bake 1 hour at 350 degrees, until golden brown.
5. Best served warm with cool whip.

Pumpkin Fudge

Servings: 12

What you need:

- 3 cups sugar
- 1/2 can evaporated milk
- 1/3 cup corn syrup
- 1/2 cup of butter
- 1/2 cup pumpkin puree
- 1 tsp pumpkin pie spice

What to do:

1. In a large saucepan over medium heat, add the pumpkin puree, pumpkin pie spice, sugar, corn syrup, and evaporated milk. Stir until simmering.
2. Cook until the mixture reaches 235-245 degrees F with a candy thermometer.
3. Remove from the heat.
4. Grease a 9x13 inch glass baking dish with butter.
5. Add the remaining butter to the fudge mixture and stir together well.
6. Pour the mixture into the greased dish and refrigerate for 2-3 hours.

PUMPKIN MUDDY BUDDIES

Servings: 10-12

What you need:

- 7 cups Chex cereal
- 1 ½ cups white chocolate
- 1 ½ cups powdered sugar
- 1 tbsp butter
- 3-4 tsp pumpkin pie spice
- Reese's pieces

What to do:

1. In a double broiler, melt butter and white chocolate chips together and stir until well combined.
2. Pour Chex cereal into a large bowl.
3. Pour half of the melted white chocolate and 2 tsp of pumpkin pie spice onto the cereal.
4. Mix it all together then pour on the rest of the chocolate and pumpkin pie spice and continue mixing until all the cereal is well coated.
5. Pour cereal and powdered sugar into a gallon sized zip lock bag.
6. Seal the bag and shake until all the cereal is coated well.
7. Toss in the Reese's pieces and shake a little more.
8. Spread it all onto a parchment paper lined baking sheet and let the mixture cool completely before serving.

Pumpkin Patch Cups

Servings: 8

What you need:

- 1 5.1-oz box instant chocolate pudding
- 3 cups milk
- 2 packages Oreos
- 1 pack gummy worms
- 1 pack pumpkin candy
- 8 clear plastic cups

What to do:

1. Whisk together the chocolate pudding mix and the milk and place it in the refrigerator.
2. Using a food processor, crush the Oreos until smooth.
3. Layer the chocolate pudding and Oreos in a clear plastic cup, make the last later an Oreo layer (Oreos, pudding, Oreos, pudding, Oreos).
4. Top with a couple pumpkin candies and a gummy worm.
5. Serve immediately or cover with plastic wrap and refrigerate until ready to serve.

PUMPKIN PreTZeIS

Servings: 10-12

What you need:

- 1 16-oz package white almond bark
- 1 tbsp shortening
- 1 bag mini pretzels
- 1 bag M&M's
- Orange food coloring

What to do:

1. Melt almond bark according to package directions but add shortening to it before melting and make sure it all combined well after its melted.
2. Add orange food coloring to the almond bark and mix well.
3. Dunk each pretzel into the almond bark then lay on a baking sheet lined with parchment paper. The pretzels should be super covered with the almond bark to where you can't see through the pretzel holes.
4. Before the chocolate dries, place a GREEN M&M sideways in the crook of each pretzel.
5. Allow the pretzels to dry and serve.

Reese's Pieces Muddy Buddies

Servings: 8-10

What you need:

- 10 cups Chex cereal
- 1 cup milk chocolate chips
- 1 cup peanut butter
- 1/3 cup butter
- 1 tsp vanilla
- 2 cups powdered sugar
- 1 1/2 cups Reese's pieces

What to do:

1. Place all of the cereal in a very large bowl.
2. In a microwave safe bowl, melt the chocolate chips, peanut butter, and butter at 20 second intervals in the microwave until mixed well and melted. Stir between each interval.
3. Pour the vanilla into the peanut butter mixture and stir well.
4. Pour the mixture over the cereal and stir until the cereal is coated.
5. Place the powdered sugar into a gallon zip lock bag.
6. Add the cereal in batches, close the bag, and shake until the cereal is coated.
7. Pour the cereal into a large bowl and toss in the Reese's Pieces.

Spider Krispies

Servings: 12

What you need:

- 6 cups Cocoa Pebbles
- ¼ cup butter
- 1 10.5-oz bag mini marshmallows
- Round cookie cutter
- Pretzel sticks, you will need about 100 sticks
- Black icing gel

What to do:

1. Spray a 9x9 inch pan with non-stick cooking spray.
2. Take out a dozen marshmallows and set aside.
3. In a large saucepan, melt butter over low heat.
4. Stir marshmallows in to melted butter until they are completely melted.
5. Remove from heat and stir in the Cocoa Pebbles.
6. Press into the prepared 9x9 inch pan.
7. Let them cool for 15-20 minutes.
8. With a cookie cutter, cut the pebbles into circles.
9. Cut the dozen marshmallows you set aside in half to where you have two shorter marshmallows.
10. Squish marshmallows onto the pebble circles to make eyes.
11. Place a dot of black icing gel into the center of each eye to make pupils.
12. Stick 4 pretzels into each side of the circle to make spider legs.

Spider Stacks

Servings: 10-12

What you need:

- 11 oz bag chocolate chips
- 11 oz bag peanut butter chips
- 12 oz bags chow mein noodles
- Candy eyes

What to do:

1. Melt chocolate and peanut butter chips in a double broiler, stirring well to mix the two kinds of chips.
2. Pour in chow mein noodles and stir carefully until they are all evenly coated.
3. Drop by spoonful onto a baking sheet lined with parchment paper.
4. Let the stacks cool for about 5 minutes and place the candy eyes in the center.
5. Let them cool completely.

Spooky Halloween Pancakes with Syrup

Servings: 6

What you need:

· 1/2 cup white sugar
· 1/2 cup brown sugar
· 2 tbsp flour
· 2 tsp cinnamon
· 1 tsp vanilla
· 1 cup water
· Black food coloring
· 2 cups Bisquick
· 1 cup milk
· 2 eggs
· 1/2 cup pumpkin puree
· 2 tbsp sugar
· 1 tsp cinnamon
· Red and yellow food coloring

What to do:

1. In a small saucepan, bring the white sugar, brown sugar, flour, cinnamon, vanilla, and water to a boil while stirring. Add enough black food coloring to make it verrry black. Stir until mixture thickens then remove from heat and set aside.

2. In a large mixing bowl, stir together the Bisquick, milk, eggs, pumpkin, sugar, cinnamon, and food coloring until well combined and bright orange.
3. Using a 1/4 cup measuring cup, pour battle onto a hot buttered griddle. Cook on each side 2-3 minutes.
4. Transfer to plates and top with black syrup and serve.

sweet cream Bat

Servings: 10-12

What you need:

- 8 oz cream cheese, softened
- 8 oz marshmallow cream
- 1/2 cup white chocolate chips
- 1 cup cocoa pebbles
- Animal Crackers, vanilla wafers, or graham crackers

What to do:

1. In a large bowl, combine cream cheese and marshmallow cream with a mixer.
2. Take 2 tbsp out of the bowl and save it for later.
3. Fold in white chocolate chips.
4. Place mixture in freezer for 30 minutes.
5. Remove mixture from freezer and spoon out onto a large piece of parchment paper.
6. Wrap parchment paper around the mixture and form into a bat shape.
7. Put it back in the freezer for about 30 minutes.
8. Pour cocoa pebbles onto a plate and roll the hardened mixture around in the cocoa pebbles until it is coated and all brown.
9. Pipe the 2 tbsp of cream cheese/marshmallow mixture you saved earlier onto the top of the bat to resemble eyes and teeth.
10. Serve with vanilla wafers, animal crackers, graham crackers, etc.

Tongues (Dried Strawberries)

Servings: 4-6

What you need:

- 2 pints fresh strawberries
- 1/2 tbsp fresh lemon juice

What to do:

1. Preheat your oven to 175 degrees F.
2. Make sure your strawberries are THOROUGHLY dried after washing.
3. Cut the stems off the strawberries and slice them into 3 slices, lengthwise.
4. Place strawberries into a bowl and toss with them lemon juice.
5. Line a baking sheet (or two baking sheets if you need two) with parchment paper.
6. Line the strawberries on a baking sheet in a single layer, not touching. You may need to use more than one sheet.
7. Place the baking sheet(s) in the oven. The total cooking time will be about 4 hours but check the strawberries every hour. Leave the oven cracked open on the 2nd and 4th hours.
8. After 2 hours, turn the strawberries over and continue cooking.
9. Let cool and place in an airtight container for storage if not eating immediately.

White Chocolate Mummy Pretzels

Servings: 18

What you need:

- 18 pretzel rods
- 12 oz white chocolate chips
- Melton's candy eyeballs (36 of them)

What to do:

1. Melt the white chocolate in your microwave.
2. Dip each pretzel in the chocolate until completely covered. Lay the pretzels on a sheet of parchment paper.
3. Drizzle the remaining chocolate over the pretzels to look like Mummy cloth.
4. Place 2 eyes at the top of each pretzel.

Ghost Pretzels

Makes 30 pretzels

What you need:

- 30 mini pretzels
- 1 cup of white chocolate chips
- 1 tsp of coconut oil
- 1 pack of Wilton candy eyeballs (small ones)

What to do:

1. Line a baking sheet with parchment paper and set it aside.
2. Melt the white chocolate and coconut oil in a microwave safe bowl for 20 seconds at a time until completely melted. Stir until smooth.
3. Dip pretzels into melted chocolate, one at a time, then shake off excess chocolate. Be sure to shake the excess chocolate out of the bottom hole of the pretzel to make it look like a mouth.
4. Place the eyes in the top two holes; add a little extra chocolate if needed.
5. Lay on the parchment paper to dry.
6. Repeat with all of the pretzels and serve or store after they are all completely dry.

Harvest Chex Mix

Servings: 10-12

What you need:

Sauce:

- 3/4 cup butter
- 3/4 cup brown sugar
- 2 tbsp vanilla extract

Mix:

- 12-oz Rice Chex cereal
- 7-oz Bugles
- 4 cups mini pretzels
- 1 cup candy corn
- 1 cup candy corn pumpkins
- 8-oz Reese's Pieces

What to do:

1. Preheat your oven to 275 degrees F.
2. In a microwave safe bowl, melt the butter then stir in the brown sugar and vanilla and whisk until smooth.
3. Add the Chex, bugles, and pretzels to a very large bowl and mix up.
4. Pour the sauce over the cereal mixture and toss gently to coat evenly.

5. Line two large baking sheets with parchment paper and divide the mixture evenly on the two baking sheets and spread out in even layers.
6. Bake for 45 minutes. Stir every 15 minutes.
7. Remove the pans from the oven and let the mix cool.
8. Once cool, place the mix back into the large bowl and add the candy corn, pumpkins, and Reese's Pieces. Toss to combine.

No Bake Peanut Butter Pumpkin Bites

Servings: 8-10

What you need:

- 3/4 cup butter, softened
- 1 cup creamy peanut butter
- 4 cups powdered sugar
- Orange gel food coloring
- Mini chocolate chips

What to do:

1. With a hand mixer in a mixing bowl, cream together the peanut butter and butter.
2. Slowly add in the powdered sugar and mix well.
3. Add the food coloring until you reach a pumpkin orange color.
4. Refrigerate for 15 minutes.
5. Using your hands, roll the dough into 1 inch balls then place them on a large parchment paper lined baking sheet.
6. Use a toothpick to make indentions down the sides of each ball to make the lines of a pumpkin.
7. Gently press a mini chocolate chip onto the top of each pumpkin for a stem.
8. Refrigerate for another 15 minutes or until ready to serve. If not serving immediately, store in an airtight container.

GhoSt BarK

Servings: 8

What you need:

- 1 bag of orange candy melts
- 1/2 cup white candy melts
- 1/4 cup black candy melts

What to do:

1. Line a baking sheet with parchment paper.
2. Place the orange candy melts in a microwave safe bowl and microwave for 30 seconds then stir and microwave again for 30 seconds and stir again. Microwave and stir again if the candy isn't completely melted and smooth.
3. Pour the melted candy onto the parchment paper and spread it out until it is about 1/3 of an inch thick.
4. Melt the white candy melts by the same method. It won't take as long since it isn't as much candy as the orange.
5. Pour dollops of the white candy onto the orange candy. This will make the ghosts. Drag the end of a wooden spoon across each dollop to form a ghost tail and arms if you want.
6. Allow the bark to cool then melt the black candy melts and use a toothpick to give each ghost eyes and a mouth.

1. Let cool completely again then break up into pieces.

ABOUT THE AUTHOR

Hannie P. Scott, Full-Time Mom and Food Blogger

Driven by her desire for cooking for others (and herself), Hannie spends a lot of time in the kitchen! She enjoys sharing her love of food with the world by creating "no-nonsense" recipe books that anyone can use to make delicious meals.

Hannie attended the University of Southern Mississippi and received a Bachelor's degree in Nutrition & Dietetics. She enjoys cooking and experimenting with food. She hopes to inspire readers and help them build confidence in their cooking. All Hannie's recipes are easy-to-prepare with easy-to-acquire ingredients.

For more recipes, cooking tips, and Hannie's blog, visit:

www.Hanniepscott.com

NOTES

NOTES

NOTES

NOTES

NOTES

NOTES

20282275R00093

Printed in Poland
by Amazon Fulfillment
Poland Sp. z o.o., Wrocław